THE LITTLE BOOK OF CHRISTMAS JOY

MAGIC CAT PUBLISHING

OPEN AN ADVENT CALENDAR

An Advent calendar makes every day special as you count down to Christmas!

Each door has a number. Find the right number and open it to see what surprise is inside. It might be chocolate, a tiny toy or a fun picture!

It's time to start the countdown. Christmas is coming!

WRITE A CHRISTMAS ACTIVITY LIST

What activities make you feel festive?

Write down a list of things you could do with your family and friends this Christmas season.

Donate toys to charity

Look at twinkling lights

Watch a Christmas movie

Visit Santa Claus

MAKE A FESTIVE PAPER WREATH

A wreath is a beautiful decoration to hang on your door at Christmastime. Here's how to make one:

1. Cut out a big circle of cardboard, then cut a smaller circle out of the middle so you have a ring.

2. Cut out leaf shapes from green paper or wrapping paper. Glue them all over the ring until it looks full.

3. Pick any decorations you'd like to add and glue them on the wreath.

4. Finally, use a loop of ribbon or string to hang it up proudly.

LIGHT A LANTERN

Lanterns mark the start of Christmas in many cultures.

Every year on 7 December, people in Colombia celebrate Día de las Velitas – 'Day of the Little Candles'. Families and neighbours fill the streets with candles and paper lanterns, creating a magical glow.

How does seeing a lantern make you feel?

MAKE A HOT CHOCOLATE

Warm milk and rich chocolate combine to create a cosy Christmas feeling in a cup.

How do you like to make your hot chocolate? With fluffy whipped cream? A striped candy cane? You could add cinnamon for an extra festive flavour.

Make a big batch to share with others.

READ A FESTIVE STORY

There are lots of festive stories for you to read and share at Christmastime.

You could read a story that you've never read before. Or you could read your favourite story to someone else.

Ask someone older than you what their favourite festive story is. Will they read it to you?

LOOK OUT FOR WINTER'S BEAUTY

There are so many beautiful things to see in nature at Christmastime.

Go for a walk around your neighbourhood and count how many seasonal delights you can find.

Take photos or draw pictures of all the things you spot to look back on all year round.

MAKE YOUR OWN CHRISTMAS CARD

Christmas is a season of giving. Why not make your own Christmas card to give to someone else?

Fold a piece of paper in half and draw a picture on the front. Perhaps it could be a Christmas tree, a snowman or Santa Claus.

Write a kind message inside, and don't forget to say Merry Christmas!

Send the card to someone you think needs some extra Christmas joy and love.

PICK YOUR CHRISTMAS TREE

If you want a Christmas tree, a tree farm is a great place to choose one! The world's biggest Christmas tree farm is in Oregon, USA. They grow about a million trees each year.

What do you think makes the perfect tree?

Tall enough to touch the ceiling?

Strong enough to hold big baubles?

Wide enough for lots of presents underneath?

LEAVE OUT YOUR SHOES

On 5 December in the Netherlands, children place their shoes by the fireplace or door for Sinterklaas. He will fill their shoes with little gifts and sweets if they leave a carrot for his horse.

The day is called Pakjesavond, which means 'present evening'.

Why not secretly leave a little treat in someone else's shoe like Sinterklaas?

PLAY A BOARD GAME

On a cold, wintry day, stay warm and cosy indoors with a board game.

A fun board game can spread some extra Christmas joy. Find one you can play with your friends, a parent or a grandparent.

What is your favourite board game to play at Christmastime?

FIND A CHRISTMAS PICKLE ORNAMENT

Pickles are sour and salty. You might not think of them when you think of Christmas. But in some parts of the USA, pickles have an important role!

A pickle ornament is secretly hung on the Christmas tree. The first person to find it wins a prize.

Could you hang a pickle decoration on your Christmas tree this year?

SEE A CHRISTMAS PANTOMINE

At Christmas, lots of people go to the theatre to enjoy a pantomime.

A pantomime is a play that is usually based on a well-known fairy tale.

It's full of jokes, songs and music, and the audience gets to join in too – cheering for the hero and booing when the villain comes on stage.

Is there a pantomime near you that you could go and see this Christmas?

VISIT A MANGER SCENE

Step into the story of Christmas!

A manger scene shows the night Jesus was born. Some use little statues, some even have real people.

Do you have a favourite character? Perhaps one day you will play a part in a nativity.

EAT FRIED CHICKEN

The food families enjoy on Christmas Day varies around the world.

Christmas dinner in the UK often includes a roast turkey and Christmas pudding. In Japan, they eat fried chicken and strawberry shortcake.

What does your family like to eat for Christmas dinner?

BUILD A SNOWMAN

When it's snowing outside, it's the perfect time to build a snowman!

1. Roll two big snowballs for the body and head.

2. Use sticks for the arms and pebbles for the face.

3. A carrot is a perfect nose.

4. Wrap up your snowman with a scarf and gloves.

GO ICE SKATING

Christmas is a merry time to go ice skating.

Some places set up an ice rink that everyone can skate on together. One of the most famous is in New York City, USA, where a big rink is set up in front of Rockefeller Center each year.

Is there an ice rink near you that you could visit this Christmas?

MAKE A CHRISTMAS TREE TOPPER

Make an angel to go on top of your Christmas tree.

1. Cut a paper plate in half.

2. Use one half to make a cone for the angel's dress. Glue in place.

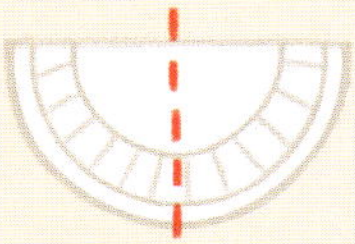

3. Take the other half and cut it in half again. These are the wings.

4. Cut a circle of paper for the face and glue on string for the hair.

5. Glue everything together. Then it's time to decorate!

FIND FIVE FESTIVE RED THINGS

Look around your house or go on a walk around your neighbourhood and try to spot five red festive items.

You could find a:

Candy cane

Poinsettia plant

Stocking

Holly berry

Santa hat

What other red things did you find?

BREAK OPEN A PIÑATA

In Mexico, breaking open a piñata kicks the festive season off with a bang!

Piñatas are usually made, and broken, during las posadas – a series of fun celebrations in the countdown to Christmas.

The piñatas are traditionally in the shape of a seven-pointed star. What shape would you choose for your piñata?

WATCH A SANTA CLAUS PARADE

Since 1905, a Santa Claus parade has kicked off the festive season in Toronto, Canada. It has marching bands, colourful floats and Santa riding on a sleigh!

Some Santa Claus parades raise money that is used to help the community.

Is there a Santa Claus parade where you live?

WEAR A CHRISTMAS JUMPER

As the weather turns colder, it's a good time to put on a jumper. How about a Christmas one?

What design will you choose?

SING A CHRISTMAS CAROL

For centuries people have sung carols to spread happiness at Christmas.

You can sing with your family, friends or on your own. It's always fun! You could even sing at a hospital to help spread Christmas cheer.

Which Christmas carol do you love to sing the most?

MAKE A MINI BEAD WREATH

Create a mini wreath using beads of all different shapes, sizes and colours – the perfect decoration for your Christmas tree.

1. Thread beads onto a pipe cleaner.

2. Bend it into a circle to make a wreath shape.

3. Tie on a ribbon so you can hang it.

Why not make one as a gift? You could use your friend's favourite colours for the beads.

DECORATE A GINGERBREAD HOUSE

Decorating a gingerbread house is a sweet Christmas activity. There are so many ways to decorate one to look extra festive.

Why not invite a friend to help you decorate your gingerbread house? Then you can enjoy eating it together!

BUNDLE UP WARM

It's nice and cosy to wear lots of layers when the frosty Christmas air sets in.

What's your favourite thing to wear that keeps you warm during winter?

A padded coat

A soft woolly hat

A long knitted scarf

Wellington boots

Fluffy mittens

WRITE A LETTER TO SANTA CLAUS

Santa loves hearing from children all around the world – but Santa won't know what's on your wish list unless you write and tell him!

Before you post your letter, write Santa's address on the envelope. Don't forget a stamp.

Include your own name and address too, so Santa knows where to deliver your presents!

DO A RANDOM ACT OF KINDNESS

One story of how Santa Claus began comes from modern-day Türkiye, where a kind Greek bishop called Saint Nicholas secretly helped those in need.

Do a random act of kindness in the spirit of St. Nicholas this Christmastime.

Give someone a compliment

Donate warm clothes

Share a festive treat

MAKE A PAPER CHAIN

Make a festive paper chain to hang from the ceiling or wrap around your Christmas tree.

You could even use leftover scraps of wrapping paper to make it.

1. Cut rectangular strips of paper, about two inches wide.

2. Take one strip and glue the ends together to make a loop.

3. Thread a new strip through the loop, then glue its ends to make another loop.

4. Keep adding strips until your chain is as long as you like!

CELEBRATE CHRISTMAS IN SUMMER!

For countries in the southern hemisphere, December is a summer month.

In Australia, Christmas celebrations might include surfing, street parties in the sunshine and barbecues on the beach.

What could you do to celebrate Christmas in summer where you live?

ATTEND A MIDNIGHT MASS SERVICE

Many Christians around the world mark Christmas by attending Midnight Mass on Christmas Eve.

The service begins at midnight and includes carols, readings and the story of Jesus's birth.

Have you ever been to Midnight Mass?
Or do you know someone who has been before?

TALK TO AN ANIMAL ON CHRISTMAS EVE

A legend from Poland says that at midnight on Christmas Eve, animals are magically able to speak.

What is your favourite animal?

What do you think it would say if it could talk?

FIND FIVE FESTIVE GREEN THINGS

Look around your house or go on a walk around your neighbourhood and try to spot five green festive items.

You could find a:

Elf hat

Fir wreath

Bauble

Christmas tree

Sprig of mistletoe

What other green things did you find?

MAKE A CHRISTMAS CARD DISPLAY

How many Christmas cards have you received so far this year? Why not turn them into a fun display?

Use string and tape to make a Christmas tree shape on a wall. Then clip your cards to the string with pegs so they hang like ornaments.

PLANT A PAPERWHITE

Paperwhites are beautiful flowers that bloom during the winter. They look lovely at Christmastime.

They're also very easy to grow indoors. You could plant some paperwhites to give to somebody as a Christmas gift.

Plant your paperwhite bulbs in a pot a few weeks before you want them to bloom.

What kind of flower do you like best?
What time of year does it grow?

LISTEN TO A TRADITIONAL TALE

There are lots of traditional Christmas stories from all around the world. This one comes from Italy.

An old woman called La Befana was visited by three wise men on their way to visit baby Jesus. They asked her to join, but she said she was too busy sweeping. Later, she changed her mind and tried to find them but got lost.

Every year on the night of 5 January, La Befana flies through the sky on her broom, leaving sweets for children in case one of them is the baby Jesus.

EAT A ROSCÓN DE REYES

A roscón de reyes is a special cake eaten in Spain on 6 January – Three Kings Day – to celebrate the day the three wise men brought gifts to baby Jesus.

It is filled with fluffy whipped cream and decorated with colourful candied fruits that look like the jewels on the kings' crowns.

There's also a tiny toy hidden inside the cake. If it's in your slice, it means you'll have a lucky year!

WRAP UP A CHRISTMAS PRESENT

Unwrapping a present is one of the most exciting parts of Christmas Day. You never know what's under the wrapping paper until you tear it open.

How will you wrap your Christmas presents this year?

In a gift bag filled with crinkly tissue paper

In a box with a shiny bow on top

In your own homemade wrapping paper

Whatever you choose, it's the thought and love that counts!

MAKE A HANDMADE GIFT

A handmade gift is the perfect way to show someone how much you care for them at Christmas.

Make a sentimental gift that comes from the heart.

Make a practical gift that you know they will love using.

Make a personal gift by adding their name to it.

Who will you make a gift for this festive season?

RUN IN A FESTIVE FUN RUN

Put on a Christmas jumper, grab a Santa hat, lace up your trainers and take part in a festive fun run.

Fun runs can be an exciting way to raise money for a good cause at Christmas.

Why not give it a try? It doesn't matter how fast you run – it's all about joining in and having fun.

VISIT A CHRISTMAS MARKET

Christmas markets are full of fun stalls selling festive treats and homemade items.

The Dresden Striezelmarkt is Germany's oldest Christmas market. You can ride on a Ferris wheel, nibble gingerbread and buy handmade decorations to take home.

Have you ever visited a Christmas market? What festive things did you buy there?

DONATE TOYS

Christmas is all about sharing joy, and one way you can do this is by making a donation.

Do you have any toys that you don't play with anymore? Why not give them a new home so that another child can enjoy them this Christmas?

Just make sure your toys are clean and ready for their next adventure.

DECORATE YOUR CHRISTMAS TREE

Fill your Christmas tree's branches with beautiful decorations that fill you with joy.

What do you like to decorate with the most?

Angel topper

Candy canes

Little bells

Shiny tinsel

Colourful lights

Glittering baubles

MAKE SALT DOUGH DECORATIONS

With just a simple salt dough, you can craft beautiful handmade Christmas ornaments.

1. Mix 250g flour, 125ml water and 125g salt to make a dough.

2. Roll out the dough and cut out shapes with cookie cutters.

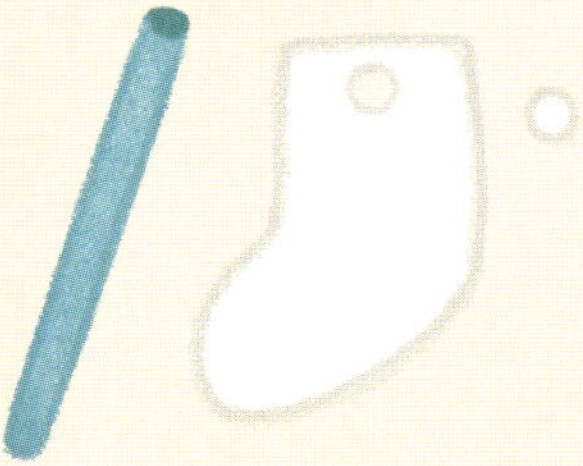

3. Use a straw to make a small hole in the top for hanging.

4. Ask a grown up to bake the ornaments at your oven's lowest temperature for 3 hours, or until hard.

5. Once cool, it's time to decorate!

FIND TWINKLING CHRISTMAS LIGHTS

At Christmas, many people decorate their homes and gardens with twinkling lights. They make the streets sparkle with a magical glow.

Take a walk around your neighbourhood with an adult after dark. How many lights can you spot? Which ones are your favourites?

GET ON SANTA'S NICE LIST

Every Christmas, Santa makes a list of all the children who have been extra kind and helpful.

Santa loves to see the little things you do every day that fill the world with Christmas cheer.

What can you do to get on Santa's nice list?

Set the table

Share your toys

Clean up

Make someone smile

WRITE YOUR CHRISTMAS LIST

It's fun to write a list of things you'd love to find under the tree on Christmas Day. You might ask for:

A warm jumper

Some craft supplies

A soft stuffed animal

An exciting book

Why not make another list of gifts you'd like to give to your friends and family? You can cross them off as you deliver the presents, just like Santa!

GO SLEDDING

One, two, three – WHEEE!

Racing down a snowy hill on a sled is so much fun. It's a great way to enjoy a wintry day outdoors with friends and family.

People have been using sleds for thousands of years – not just for fun but also to carry supplies, like firewood, over snow and ice.

MAKE AN ADVENT WREATH

An Advent wreath is used by Christians to count down to Christmas Day.

You can make your own with pipe cleaners!

1. Wrap green pipe cleaners around a pencil, then slide them off and join together for the wreath.

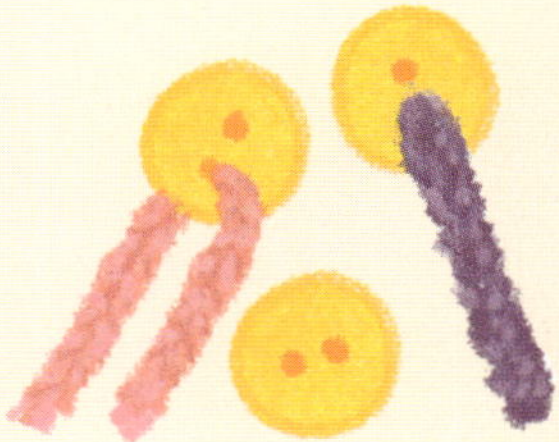

2. Thread a yellow button onto one pink and three purple pipe cleaners to be the lit candles.

3. Fold each pipe cleaner in half, twist to secure the button and then curl the ends around the green wreath to attach.

STARGAZE LIKE LOS REYES MAGOS

In many Spanish-speaking countries, the three wise men are called los Reyes Magos. According to the Christmas story, they followed a bright star to the town of Bethlehem to welcome baby Jesus.

When you look up at the night sky, what stars or constellations can you spot? The North Star? Orion's Belt? There are so many twinkling above.

READ A POEM ON CHRISTMAS EVE

'Twas the night before Christmas,
when all through the house,
Not a creature was stirring,
not even a mouse

These are the opening lines to 'A Visit from St. Nicholas'. It's a classic Christmas poem about an exciting visit from Santa and his reindeer on Christmas Eve.

Do you know the names of Santa's reindeer? Will they visit you on Christmas Eve?

MAKE A SNOW ANGEL

If you're lucky enough to be somewhere snowy at Christmas, you could make a snow angel.

1. Lie down on your back and sweep your arms up and down to make wings.

2. Move your legs in and out to make a long robe.

3. Carefully stand up and admire the outline of your magical snow angel!

EAT A FISH DISH

Some Italian Americans celebrate the night before Christmas with a special tradition called the Feast of the Seven Fishes.

Families gather for a big meal made up of seven different fish and seafood dishes.

They eat things like:

Seafood pasta

Whole roasted cod

Octopus salad

Calamari

What is your favourite food?
Could you eat it seven times in one meal?

MAKE YOUR OWN WRAPPING PAPER

Make your gifts extra joyful by creating your own wrapping paper!

Start with some plain brown paper, then decorate it with markers, crayons, stamps or paints.

Will you draw stripes? Polka dots? Little Christmas trees or yummy candy canes?

Don't forget to let it dry before you wrap your Christmas gift!

LEARN HOW TO SAY 'MERRY CHRISTMAS'

Discover how people wish each other a Merry Christmas in different languages – a fun way to share festive cheer across the world.

Joyeux Noël!

French

Feliz Navidad!

Spanish

Buon Natale!

Italian

Srećan Božić!

Serbian

Wesołych Świąt!

Polish

圣诞快乐
shèng dàn kuài lè!

Chinese

FIND FIVE FESTIVE BLUE THINGS

Look around your house or go on a walk around your neighbourhood and try to spot five blue festive items.

You could find a:

Snowflake

Frozen puddle

Bag of sweets

Roll of wrapping paper

Piece of tinsel

What other blue things did you find?

WEAR CHRISTMAS PYJAMAS AND WATCH A MOVIE

Watching a Christmas movie is a cosy way to spend a wintry evening.

Put on matching Christmas pyjamas with your family, then snuggle up to watch something festive.

What's your favourite Christmas movie? Ask your parents or grandparents what Christmas movies they watched when they were your age.

PLAY A GAME OF CHRISTMAS CHARADES

Charades is a fun game that is played without saying a single word!

Think of a film, book, animal or activity and silently act it out so your teammates can guess what it is.

Here are some Christmassy ideas to get you started:

Building a snowman

A reindeer

The Nutcracker ballet

What other Christmas things could you act out?

MAKE A SANTA FACE

Create a cute Santa decoration with a paper plate, cotton wool and pens.

1. Colour two-thirds of the plate for Santa's face, and the top third red for his hat.

2. Glue on cotton wool for his beard and his hat's fluffy trim.

3. Draw on eyes and a nose to finish his face.

Hide your Santa face with a kind note – a secret Santa surprise for someone to find!

BAKE FESTIVE SUGAR COOKIES

Ingredients:

- 150g caster sugar
- 150g unsalted butter
- 1 medium egg
- 2 tsps vanilla extract
- 280g plain flour
- 1 tsp baking powder
- A pinch of salt

Method:

1. Heat the oven to 190°C or 170°C fan.
2. Beat sugar and butter until fluffy. Then mix in eggs and vanilla extract.
3. Add flour, baking powder and salt to form a soft dough.
4. Roll out the dough until it's 1cm thick.
5. Cut out your cookies and bake for 7-10 minutes on a baking sheet lined with parchment paper.
6. Once completely cool, decorate your cookies (you can make a simple icing with icing sugar and water).

HELP AN ANIMAL DURING WINTER

Frosty winter weather can be hard on creatures living outside at Christmas.

Here are some kind things you can do to help them.

Donate extra blankets to an animal shelter.

Put up or clean out nest boxes.

Fill a bird feeder.

Make a woodpile where wildlife can shelter.

GIFT A BOOK ON CHRISTMAS EVE

A book is a fantastic Christmas present to give or receive.

In Iceland, there's even a special tradition called Jólabókaflóðið – the 'Christmas book flood'. On Christmas Eve, families exchange books, then curl up together to read their new treasures.

What is your favourite book to read? Who would you like to share it with?

DECORATE WITH A YULE GOAT

In old Swedish tales, elves were said to ride a Yule goat to deliver presents to children at Christmastime.

Today, Yule goats are made from straw and hung as festive decorations.

Do you have an animal ornament on your Christmas tree?

MAKE A PAPER SNOWFLAKE

Bring a touch of winter indoors with a paper snowflake. Here's how to make one:

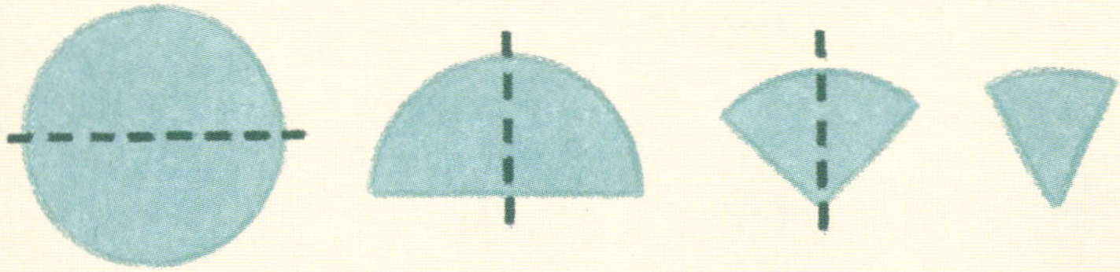

1. Cut a piece of paper into a circle. Fold it in half three times to make a thin triangle.

2. Cut small shapes out of the edges of the triangle.

3. Unfold the paper to reveal your snowflake.

Each snowflake will be a different shape, just like how real snowflakes are all unique.

GO ROLLER SKATING

In some countries, Christmas means ice skating, skiing or sledding.

But in Venezuela, families celebrate by roller skating through the streets to attend Midnight Mass. This tradition is called las patinatas, which means 'the skating'.

Do you have a special way of getting around at Christmastime?

DANCE TO *THE NUTCRACKER*

The Nutcracker is a famous ballet that is performed all over the world at Christmas.

It was written by a Russian composer called Pyotr Tchaikovsky, and it tells the story of a little girl named Clara and her magical nutcracker toy that comes to life one Christmas Eve.

Put on some music from *The Nutcracker* and dance along! How does the music make you feel?

MAKE A CHRISTMAS ORNAMENT MEMORY

Create an ornament to hang on your Christmas tree that reminds you of a special memory from the year.

1. Draw a picture of your special memory.

2. Wrap your picture in clear sticky tape to keep it safe.

3. Use a hole punch to make a hole in the top of your picture.

4. Thread ribbon or string through the hole for hanging.

VISIT SANTA

Santa and his helpers enjoy visiting towns and meeting children before Christmas.

You can say hello to the elves, tell Santa what you want for Christmas and have a special photo taken.

Where can you visit Santa near you?
What will you ask him for?

PERSONALIZE A CHRISTMAS STOCKING

Children once hung regular socks for Santa to fill. Today, stockings are made from all kinds of fabrics – from felt to velvet.

Why not create your own unique stocking? Start with a plain one and add your own decorations.

Glue on decorations.

Cut letters from felt to spell your name.

Use fabric pens to draw festive designs.

PULL A CRACKER AND TELL A CHRISTMAS JOKE

It's always fun to pull a Christmas cracker with a friend. They break open with a bang and contain a small toy, a paper crown and a funny joke, like:

What do you get when you cross a snowman
with a vampire?
Frostbite!

Who says "Oh! Oh! Oh!"?
Santa Claus walking backwards!

FIND FIVE FESTIVE YELLOW THINGS

Look around your house or go on a walk around your neighbourhood and try to spot five yellow festive items.

You could find a:

Gingerbread biscuit

Star-shaped tree topper

String of lights

Glowing candle

Golden bell

What other yellow things did you find?

SING *THE TWELVE DAYS OF CHRISTMAS*

The Twelve Days of Christmas is a well-loved English Christmas carol. From a partridge in a pear tree to twelve drummers drumming, each verse adds something new and fun to remember.

Sing along – and point to the gifts as you go!

MAKE A STRING OF CHRISTMAS ANGELS

Create your own string of paper angels to display as a Christmas decoration.

1. Fold an A4 piece of paper in half three times to make a thin strip.

2. Along the folded edge, draw the outline of half an angel. You could use this template to help.

3. Cut around your outline, then unfold the paper to reveal your chain of angels. Colour and decorate each one to make them unique.

SHARE A MEAL TOGETHER

All around the world, Christmas is a time for family and friends to gather for a special meal.

In the Philippines, people might share spring rolls and roasted pig. In Kenya, it could be hearty beef stew, while in the UK, it's often roast turkey.

Wherever you are, being together matters most.

Who do you most look forward to seeing at your Christmas table?

LEAVE A TREAT FOR SANTA. . .

On Christmas Eve, Santa works hard to deliver gifts to children around the world. In return, children leave out treats to keep Santa going on his journey.

A mince pie in the UK

Milk and cookies in the USA

A bowl of porridge in Sweden

Fruit cake in Chile

What treat will you leave for Santa this Christmas?

. . . AND LEAVE A TREAT FOR REINDEER TOO!

Reindeer love carrots, but for an extra-special Christmas surprise, why not make your own reindeer treats?

Combine wild birdseed, a few rolled oats, some dried fruit, and a little bit of grated cheese. Then sprinkle outside or leave in a bowl.

Reindeer treats are safe for birds to eat as well. They'll appreciate the extra food during the cold winter months.

DRAW SANTA CLAUS

Santa Claus looks different for every child, depending on where they live in the world.

For you, he might have a white beard and red suit, flying through the sky in a sleigh pulled by reindeer.

In Hawai'i, Santa wears a Hawaiian shirt and rides a canoe pulled by dolphins! In Kenya, Santa travels by camel to deliver gifts.

Now it's your turn to draw your own Santa. Why not turn your drawing into a Christmas card?

HANG UP YOUR CHRISTMAS STOCKING

On Christmas Eve, don't forget to hang up your stocking so that Santa can find it.

In the UK, stockings can be hung above a fireplace.

In Brazil, stockings are left by an open window.

In some countries, like Portugal and Vietnam, children leave out their shoes instead of stockings.

Where do you hang up your Christmas stocking? Are you excited for Santa Claus to visit on Christmas Eve?

MAGIC CAT PUBLISHING

The Little Book of Christmas Joy © 2026 Lucky Cat Publishing Ltd
Written by Thea Bevan
Illustrations © 2026 Annelies Draws
First Published in 2026 by Magic Cat Publishing, an imprint of Lucky Cat Publishing Ltd, Unit 2 Empress Works, 24 Grove Passage, London E2 9FQ, UK
EU Authorised Representative Magic Cat Publishing, an imprint of Lucky Cat Publishing Ltd, PAKTA svetovanje d.o.o., Stegne 33, Ljubljana, Slovenia

A catalogue record for this book is available from the British Library.

ISBN 978-1-917768-23-8

The illustrations were drawn in coloured pencil
Set in Annelies Pen, Quicksand and Sofa Sans

Published by Rachel Williams and Jenny Broom
Designed by Nicola Price and Ashtyn Botterill
Edited by Helen Brown

Manufactured in China

1 3 5 7 9 8 6 4 2

FSC
www.fsc.org
MIX
Paper | Supporting responsible forestry
FSC® C109093